A VISUAL RECORD OF AUSTRALIA

ON ONE HISTORIC DAY

1.1.2000

A FOOTPRINT IN HISTORY

Midnight. SYDNEY, NSW

Random House Australia Pty Ltd
20 Alfred Street, Milsons Point, NSW 2061
http://www.randomhouse.com.au

Sydney   New York   Toronto
London   Auckland   Johannesburg

First published by Random House, 2000

Copyright © J.M. McGregor Pty Ltd 2000, and on behalf of participating photographers

National Library of Australia
Cataloguing-in-Publication Entry

    1.1.2000: 24 hours in the life of Australia.

    ISBN 0 091 84190 9

1. Australia – Pictorial works.   2. Twenty-first century.
3. Australia – Social life and customs – 1900 – .
I. Title: 1st January 2000. II. Title: 1 January 2000.

    994 070222

Conceived and produced for the publishers by
J.M. McGregor Pty Ltd, PO Box 6990, Gold Coast Mail Centre, Queensland 9726.

Originator, Producer and Editor-in-Chief: Malcolm McGregor
Print Consultant and Coordinator: Mark Garner
Editor: Jeannie McGregor
Design and Artwork: Garner Graphics, Southern Highlands
Film Processing: ColourChrome Laboratories, Sydney
Colour separation and Film: Independent Litho, Sydney
Printed in China by Everbest Printing Co Ltd

10 9 8 7 6 5 4 3 2 1

Participating photographers used FUJI films.

1.1.2000

24 hours in the life of

AUSTRALIA

RANDOM HOUSE AUSTRALIA

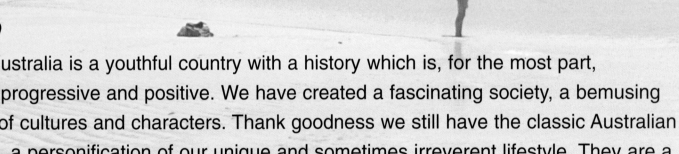

*A*ustralia is a youthful country with a history which is, for the most part, progressive and positive. We have created a fascinating society, a bemusing range of cultures and characters. Thank goodness we still have the classic Australian larrikin, a personification of our unique and sometimes irreverent lifestyle. They are a counterbalance to the inevitable pomposity which can develop in a healthy society and we are all part of the massive social spectrum illustrated in this book.

Photography, an art form which is only a little younger than Australia, has been part of our society, recording our history, for well over 150 years. A pioneer photographer was even featured on one of our banknotes. Some say that is an irony as photographers have, by and large, shunned wealth in favour of artistic freedom!

In this book we see Australians in their characteristic carefree mode celebrating the expectations of the new century – a celebration which swept around the world at the speed of sunrise. Australia, never a country to miss a good party, gained not only the winning vote for the very best millennium celebration but was fortunate enough to

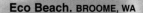
Eco Beach. BROOME, WA

have the world's most talented photographers record it. I don't say that lightly. It is not generally known that our country is home to, per capita, the highest number of winners of World Press Photo Awards – the annual grand prix of photo-reportage hosted in Europe. These photojournalists – visual nomads – generally work for the world's leading magazines. On this day many came home and turned on their talent for us to enjoy. Who could argue with the results which, in the space of 24 hours, encapsulated the continuing high spirits and optimism of a very young country? Who could argue with the lady in Kalgoorlie (page38) who encouraged us to start the New Year with a bang?

I hope you enjoy this lively record of our first day in the 21st century as much as I have. I hope our descendants will enjoy it in a hundred years' time, studying our mysterious rituals. I also hope that we will have managed to maintain a country which they will love as much as we do.

Janet Holmes á Court

1.1.2000 - the first light of the new millennium in the world. Qantas flight 2903 over the South Pole with Captain John Denis (left) and Captain Peter J. Smith.
ANTARCTICA

Florence H. Houghton of Melbourne on Qantas Flight 2903. At the age of 95, she has indulged in adventures most people half her age would not attempt. ANTARCTICA

■ Midnight every New Year sees several hundred guests at Chateau Hornsby Winery pick and stomp grapes for the new vintage.
ALICE SPRINGS, NT

ROBERT GRAY

■ Rave party at
Smithfield. CAIRNS, QLD

■ ACT Chief Minister
Kate Carnell (second from
right) and Chief Executive
of Koomari, Margaret
Spalding (third from right)
with friends, toasting the
success of the Koomari
Charity Ball at Parliament
House. CANBERRA, ACT

GRAHAM GITTINS

Dancing the night away at 'NY2K' dance party at the Queen's Theatre. ADELAIDE, SA

PETER HASSON

■ Brooke Lamb and friend at the Nippon Inn Nightclub. BROOME, WA

TONY BEE

■ Jessica and Leo at the Bachelors and Spinsters Ball, which was attended by around 4,000 people. "The utes are all lined up and we hear the engines roar – broom broom. Doesn't that sound give you goosebumps!" GUNNEDAH, NSW

TONY BEE

■ Bachelors and Spinsters Ball – Renae and Peter. GUNNEDAH, NSW

SORREL WILBY

■ 12:35am: Sydney Lord Mayor, Frank Sartor (right), and Syd Hammond, celebrate the success of the fireworks display. SYDNEY, NSW

Paul Melmeth from Newcastle on Qantas Flight 2903 over the South Pole. ANTARCTICA

MICHAEL LANGFORD

2:00am: The 'Blues Brothers' party on! SYDNEY, NSW

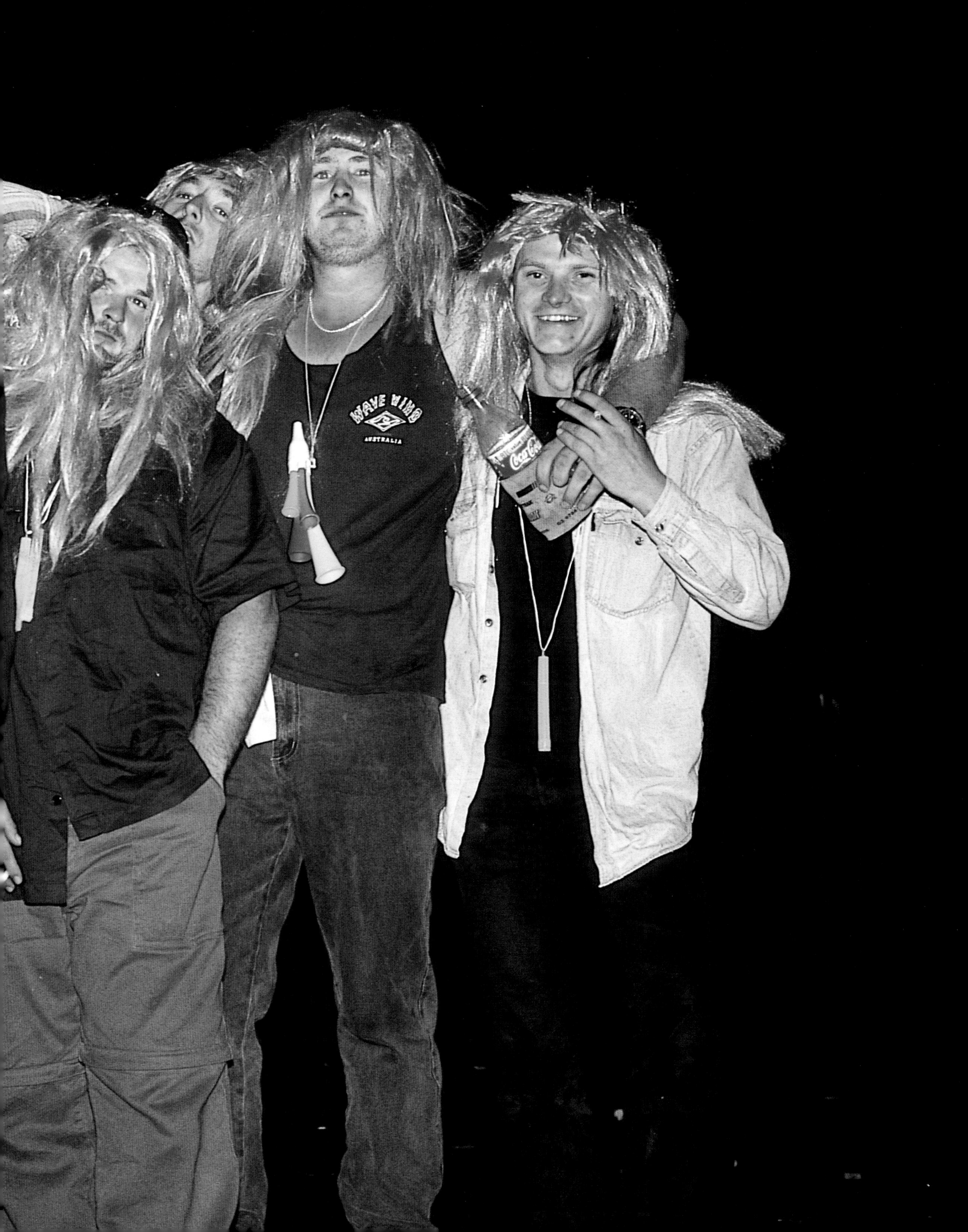

■ One way of
ensuring a good seat!
Crystal Brook – 'Dawn
2000' Music Gathering.
SOUTHERN FLINDERS
RANGES, SA

■ Teenage band
'Finger Box' entertain at
Main Street Party, Town
Square. BROKEN HILL, NSW

Carmen Miranda? BROOME, WA

DANIEL LINET

■ Wise move! Party goers voluntarily check their blood alcohol level at the police station. BROKEN HILL, NSW

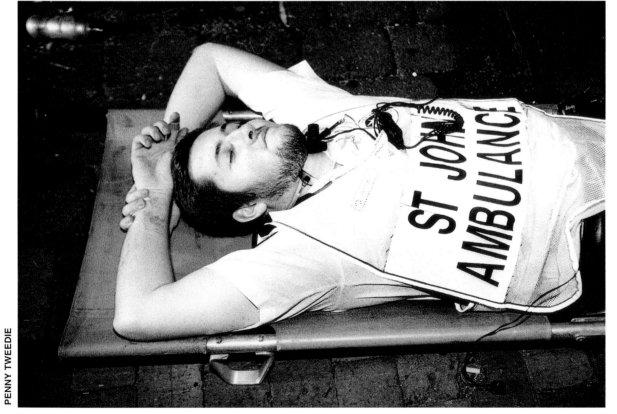

PENNY TWEEDIE

■ Exhausted. SYDNEY, NSW

PENNY TWEEDIE

■ St John's Ambulance volunteers work on a patient injured at the Rocks. SYDNEY, NSW

■ Celebration at RIO's nightclub. KATHERINE, NT

ROGER GARWOOD

■ Local lads at the unveiling ceremony of a new clock for the Menzies Town Hall. MENZIES, WA

■ Miss Ballina float from Byron Bay street parade. BYRON BAY, NSW

■ 12:55am: Bedded down for the night in the shearing shed (l to r: Rosemary Leahy, Catherine Ryan, Christina Leahy, Sarah Ryan).
SPRING PLAINS, VIC

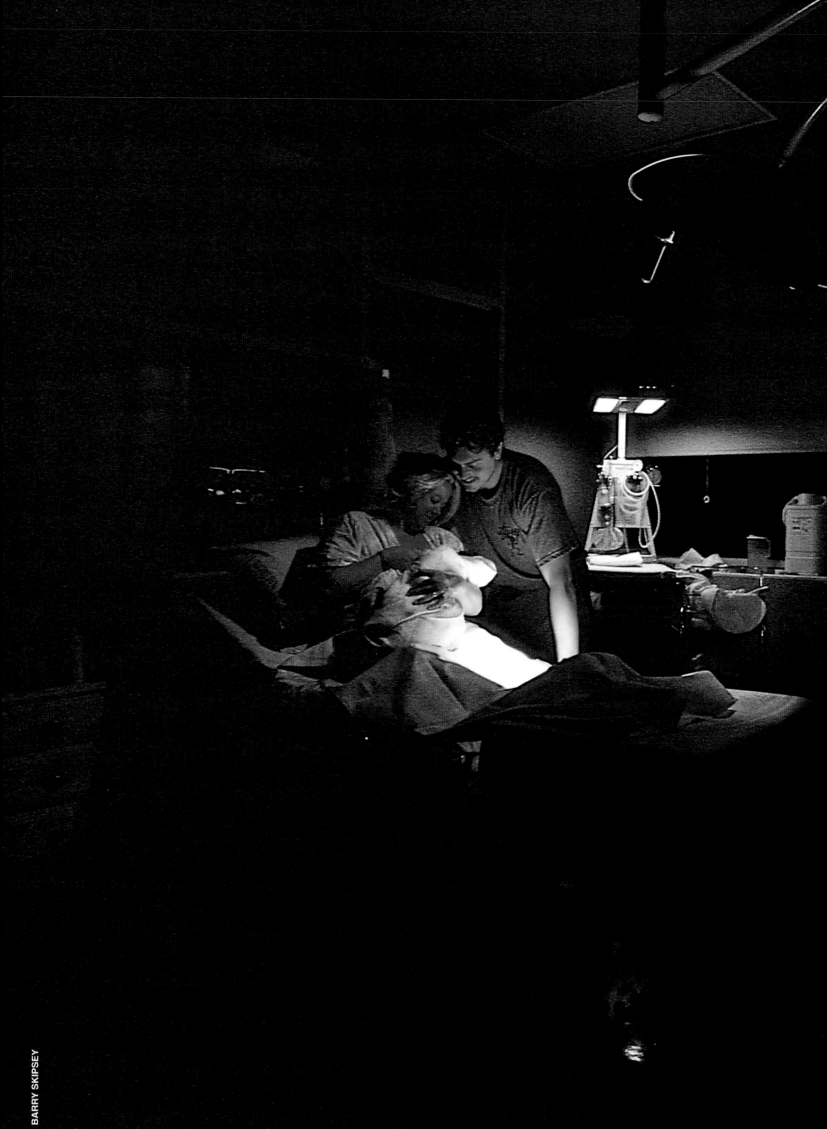

Millennium baby –
30 minutes old,
born 3:30am 1.1.2000
at Alice Springs
Hospital, Jahmaine
Rita Dew with parents
Natalie Dew and Craig
Sheridan.
ALICE SPRINGS, NT

LYN WHITFIELD-KING

■ Kim Beazley, Leader of the Opposition, relaxes with Dr Christor Chung and sleepy Julian Chung. PERTH, WA

■ Sue Cowling, Nurse Unit Manager at St Vincents Hospital, with a patient who had to be restrained and who stopped breathing twice. MELBOURNE, VIC

ROB WALLS

■ Some of the Danish crew members of 'Nokia', the yacht that won line honours and set a new record for the Sydney to Hobart yacht race. HOBART, TAS

■ 1:00am: Year 2000 National Co-ordination Centre. Senator Ian Campbell with operators Cathy Ellis and Jonathon Abrahams in the monitoring and responding room. At midnight the lights stayed on, no financial institution systems failed and no aircraft fell from the sky. A team of 40 people working in shifts operated the monitoring room and a new record was created for the number of visits to a web site – more than 5.3 million visits from around the world were recorded during the first seven hours of the new year. Government, companies and institutions spent $12 billion in checking and cleansing computer systems. CANBERRA, ACT

The odd couple! Alex Gilmour McDonald and Joe Guy, the Millennium Robot Man, at Dubbo Golf Club, DUBBO, NSW

ROGER GARWOOD

■ As he has done for
as long as he can
remember, Bill Bond
raises the Australian flag
outside his bush camp
at sunrise. Known as the
Duke of Dingo Creek, Bill
has been prospecting for
many years. He spent
time in the Klondyke and
became a good friend of
John Wayne, joining him
and Debbie Reynolds for
holidays in Acapulco.
DINGO CREEK, WA

MATT NETTHEIM

■ Crystal Brook –
'Dawn 2000' Music
Gathering. SOUTHERN
FLINDERS RANGES, SA

MICHAEL COYNE

■ 5:30am: Farmer John Farley at 'Kilmuir'. DERRINAL, VIC

■ Nikki studied psychology but didn't like it! The Cresta Casa.
KALGOORLIE, WA

See it in with a Bang

■ On guard! RAAF base at dawn – police dog Sal with handler Shane Johnston and United Nations C130 Hercules, present because of the Timor crisis. DARWIN, NT

ROB WALLS

■ 5:15am: Mt Wellington as the sun first touches Australia. Grant Maddock has an appreciative audience in his dogs Zoetje and Ratu as he serenades the first light of the new millennium on South American bamboo flutes. HOBART, TAS

■ Looking across Dickson's Inlet towards Mossmans Gorge and the Rex Range.
PORT DOUGLAS, QLD

DANIEL LINET

■ 5:45am: Rosalee Webb is a psychologist working at the sexual assault and emergency clinic at Broken Hill Hospital. Since her father died on New Year's Day 1993, Rosalee takes the time to remember him every New Year's morning. "My father is the first thing I think of at the start of each new year. I find this very comforting." BROKEN HILL, NSW

DOUG SPOWART

■ John Elliott at Gowrie Mountain on the Darling Downs. Elliott, writer, publisher and photographer, covers issues related to Australian and international country music. He spends most of his time on the road.
DARLING DOWNS, QLD

MICHAEL COYNE

■ 6:00am: Farmer Tony Leahy. MIA MIA, VIC

■ Four Mile Beach.
PORT DOUGLAS, QLD

ROBERT GRAY

A grandstand view of the new
millennium for Mark Foote and
Sharon Mayes. TOWN BEACH, WA

First light for Jenny
Beech and Lyndon
Oats. PALM COVE, QLD

■ First light at
Cape Byron lighthouse.
BYRON BAY NSW

■ 'Paradise Bird Man' – Davvyd Brown, a major tourist attraction
on the Gold Coast for the last 20 years. KURRAWA BEACH, QLD

■ Cleaning up after Australia's biggest party – City Care workers, Mick Hanshaw (left) and Les Downey. SYDNEY, NSW

■ Every kid's dream!
KALLISTA, VIC

FAR RIGHT
■ Alex Page, born 1.1.92, is less than impressed at the start to his eighth birthday as piper Ross Redwin welcomes the first morning of the new millennium with a stirring rendition of 'Scotland the Brave'. LYONVILLE, VIC

Will today be the day? Laurie Hanson works his detector over the ground a few kilometres outside Kookynie. In the background is the headframe of the old Altona Mine which was a major gold producer at the turn of the century. KOOKYNIE, WA

■ Still ready to party
after a long night.
BROADBEACH, QLD

■ Henning Hintze sells
tropical flowers,
haliconias and gingers,
at the Parap Markets.
DARWIN, NT

GARY LEWIS

Elated by the dawn of a new century outside Flinders Street Station.
MELBOURNE, VIC

■ Christos Raskatos
of Lorne Fisheries on
the Lorne Pier. Well
known, Chris writes
poems, pop philosophy
and commentary on a
board outside his fish
shop, which sells local
fish from Apollo Bay
and Portland. LORNE, VIC

RENNIE ELLIS

■ Market gardeners set
up their stalls for the
weekly Salamanca
Market. HOBART, TAS

ROB WALLS

■ Margie Magee washes sweet potatoes at Greenwood Farm, which the Grills family have worked for over a century. WINFIELD, QLD

PETER O'HALLORAN

■ Warren Sneesby inspects lucerne at his property 'Glen Oak'. WALLABADAH, NSW

■ Participants camp at the rodeo. UPPER HORTON, NSW

MONICA NAPPER

■ Joyce Smart on her property, where she does all the farm work. Joyce has been associated with cows for some decades. At the age of 12 she rescued a drowning calf from a water hole, administered artificial respiration, loaded the calf onto a wheelbarrow and carted it home. The owner decided to destroy the calf but Joyce persuaded him to give it to her. This was the start of her herd of cows and today at 70 she has around 80 head of livestock. PROSPECT HILL, SA

■ Breakfast in Kings Park. PERTH, WA

Cha cha cha! Outside the Treasury Casino, the rhythm of Latin American music captivates people enjoying a sausage sizzle provided by the casino and Radio Station Triple M. BRISBANE, QLD

ANDREW CHAPMAN

■ Fireman Peter Stowell with Loco 14a. BELGRAVE, VIC

■ The ultimate train set! Puffing Billy Railway is run by a largely volunteer group of people interested in narrow–gauge steam railways. The railway line is 15 miles long and travels through picturesque hillside country from Belgrave to Gembrook. Firemen Ron Kain and Geoff Schmidt. BELGRAVE STATION, VIC

■ **Angel of the morning?** SURFERS PARADISE, QLD

TIM GEORGESON

■ Main street.
NIMBIN, NSW

■ After a night overseeing celebrations, Kevin Pusey, Vice President of Menzies Shire, decides on a 'hair of the dog' at breakfast. He shares a sparkling Shiraz with wife Margaret and prospector Laurie Hanson. At the turn of the century, this building was a row of shops including a general store and butcher. Kevin and Margaret renovated the building and now use it as a home plus small museum. KOOKYNIE, WA

ROGER GARWOOD

71

■ Ella Havelka (11) performs the Brolga Dance at the Terra Mungamine Reserve on the banks of the Macquarie River. The grinding grooves on the outcrop of sandstone are believed to be 15,000 years old. DUBBO, NSW

■ The Reverend Gloria Shipp, priest in charge of the Koori Anglican Fellowship at St Lukes Anglican Church. DUBBO, NSW

MERV BISHOP

MERV BISHOP

■ The Prime Minister is entitled to a day off from running the country. John Howard, at Kirribilli House. SYDNEY, NSW

PHILIP GOSTELOW

■ Sir William Deane, Governor General of Australia, with a group of children who stayed overnight at Admiralty House. L to r: Serene Halawani, Nyree Manning, Sir William Deane, Paul Sanderson and Nicholas Ryden.

Above, some of the children have just woken and are sitting under the colonnades. All the children are either recent recipients of, or waiting to receive, kidney or liver transplants. They watched the fireworks over the harbour and slept in sleeping bags on the ground floor. KIRRIBILLI, NSW

GRAHAM BURSTOW

GRAHAM BURSTOW

■ Street performers
outside the Treasury
Casino. BRISBANE, QLD

TONY LEWIS

MOVE YOURSELF 1030

■ The party's over!
Victoria Square.
ADELAIDE, SA

■ Stormy Summers – Madam. After a career as a professional dancer, Stormy became the successful owner of nightclubs in Adelaide and Perth. At the age of 32 she opened her first Stormy's Bordello and over the years as a madam, she has become an Adelaide icon with her name known throughout the state. At the start of 2000, Stormy surprised South Australians with her decision to run for Lord Mayor of Adelaide. It seems her decision is more about lobbying MPs to decriminalise prostitution than an aspiration to take office. ADELAIDE, SA

MONICA NAPPER

■ A handful at any time! Meekins brothers, Blake, Joshua, Logan and Jack, on the steps of the GPO. ADELAIDE, SA

RACHEL HARRIS

BILL BACHMAN

ROEL LOOPERS

DAVID HANCOCK

ABOVE LEFT
■ "The solar panel's for the fridge." Solar–powered tepee constructed by Trisha Neate and Paul Colwell, at the Earthcore Festival in Mountain Bay.
LAKE EILDON, VIC

ABOVE RIGHT
■ Cottesloe Beach.
PERTH, WA

LEFT
■ Peter Roper, Stevedoring Manager with Rooney Shipping and Trading, oversees loading of equipment onto a vessel bound for Australian peace–keeping forces in East Timor. DARWIN, NT

Name–day service at St Nectarios Greek Orthodox Church. BURWOOD, NSW

BRIAN CASSEY

■ Shingara Singh reads from the 'Guru Granth Sahiv' (Guru-writings) at a special service at the Guru Gobind Singh Sikh Temple. GORDONVALE, QLD

■ Cooling off in the Todd River on a rare occasion that it actually contains water.
L to r: Brendan Foster, Michael Foster and Jake Carmichael. ALICE SPRINGS, NT

PETER HASSON

■ A new meaning to 'collecting the eggs'! Malcolm Douglas runs the Broome Crocodile Park and is well known throughout Australia and overseas for his TV programmes. Most of the crocodiles he has captured were pests in local river areas and the largest, 8 metres, was threatening tourists. BROOME, WA

STUART OWEN–FOX

■ Mark Swindells from Alice Springs lives at Curtain Springs Station. He left Carnarvon, WA, on 5 April 1999 on a solo trip across Australia with four camels, Rajah Red, Sydney, Murphy Satchmo and Apollo D9. He arrived in Byron Bay just before New Year's Eve. It is thought to be the first solo crossing of Australia by camel. BYRON BAY, NSW

Greeting the dawn of a new century at Tyagarah Nudist Beach. Friends on an east coast tour in an old green schoolbus called 'Gunna' explain the name: "Ya' know, one day we're gunna do this or gunna do that, or gunna travel and have fun... now we're gunna go for a swim." NEAR BYRON BAY, NSW

■ Up to their necks in it! RABY BAY, QLD

■ Toddler attempting to
bury a millennium time
capsule. ST KILDA BEACH, VIC

■ Broken Head Beach.
NORTHERN NSW

TIM GEORGESON

■ On patrol – and saving lives. KURRAWA BEACH, QLD

■ Brighton Beach. MELBOURNE, VIC

RICHARD CAMPION

GARY LEWIS

■ Removing the salt and the sand, Rebecca Taylor and son Ethan. GOLD COAST, QLD

Popular sausage sizzle outside the Treasury Casino – sponsored by the casino and Triple M Radio Station. BRISBANE, QLD

DAVID SIMMONDS

TERRY KNIGHT

■ Cliff Young, 77 years old, dairy and potato farmer and marathon runner. His next race will be a 1000 mile run in April 2000 at Coburg and he plans to be competing at least until he turns 80. KAWARREN, VIC

■ Lord Mayor of Darwin, George Brown and wife Noreen in their back yard. George Brown is a part of Darwin. He is a much loved and outspoken protector of planning and environmental issues and is credited with masterminding much of the park–like beauty that is a feature of the city today. DARWIN, NT

BRIAN CASSEY

ROB WALLS

■ Joyce Atkinson, 100 years old, was born in Ingham. She and her family moved to Cashmere Cattle Station near Mt Garnet in 1903. ATHERTON, QLD

■ Born in 1898, Ida Wood, Rita Harland and Kathleen Rowbottom, have lived in three centuries. Their collective memories include tall ships and carrier pigeons, shipwrecks and the arrival of cars in Tasmania. HOBART, TAS

The MacKenzie and Robertson families appreciate the beauty and solitude of the Australian bush as they enjoy a barbecue picnic.
DANDENONG RANGES, VIC

Singh family BBQ, Aussie style. Are the pigs worried?
John Singh's Punjab Stud, known throughout Australia
for its production of high quality, pure-bred pigs, has
been run as a family business since 1975. COORABELL, NSW

Olympic City. Darling Harbour, SYDNEY, NSW

■ Smoko at the 'crib room' – George Appleton, underground serviceman at Kundana Mine. KALGOORLIE, WA

■ A good samaritan.
TOOWOOMBA, QLD

GRAHAM BURSTOW

■ Terry Grimison,
long time truck driver,
with cattle road train.
KATHERINE, NT

ANDREW MATHIESON

■ Royal Flying Doctor –
Dr Peter Lyall strapped in
ready for takeoff on an
emergency call. He will
maintain radio contact with
the patient throughout the
trip. BROKEN HILL, NSW

■ At Peaceful Gardens in Nerrena, Isaac Robson works Amber the draught horse. Amber is an integral part in the choice of low impact farming methods, reducing the high costs of fuel, tractor parts and machine maintenance. Amber allows everything to slow down to a pace that permits closer observation of the health of the fruit trees. SOUTH GIPPSLAND, VIC

CAROLYN JOHNS

■ Wendy Schafer and friend at Lagoon Crocodile Farm. DARWIN, NT

■ John – farm hand. WINFIELD, QLD

DAVID HANCOCK

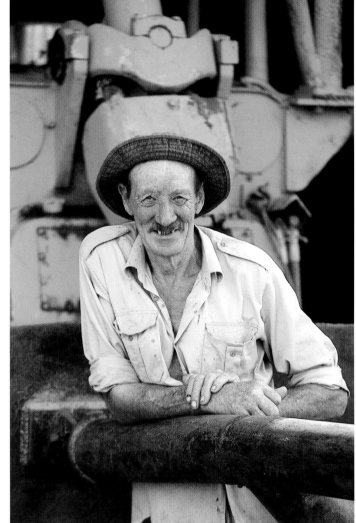

PETER O'HALLORAN

■ The Cairns to Kuranda scenic rail train stops at Barron Falls. In the 'wet', these falls present an impressive, roaring torrent. KURANDA, QLD

ROBERT GRAY

JOANNE FELK

■ The joy of living! Katrina Rutherford finds sunflowers growing beside the road at WILLOWTREE, NSW

■ Elders Rorani and Buetts of the Church of Jesus Christ Latter Day Saints. KALGOORLIE, WA

■ Little girl, big statue! Mia Andersen in contemplative mood. BERKELEY, NSW

SORREL WILBY

SORREL WILBY

■ At the Fo Guang Shan Nan Tien Temple, the new millennium (according to the western calendar) is celebrated with a lion dance (left).

Lisa Tang and Kwan Chung eat fairy floss before a dance performance at the temple. BERKELEY, NSW

SORREL WILBY

Rodeo is alive and well if Tumbarumba is the measure! The Tumbarumba Rodeo attracts some 3,000 spectators every New Year's Day. On the southern slopes of the Snowy Mountains, Tumbarumba is largely untouched by the modern world. The word Tumbarumba is thought to be derived from the Wiradjuri aboriginal language, meaning 'sounding ground'. It is believed there are places in the district that give off a hollow sound when hit. TUMBARUMBA, NSW

GRAHAM GITTINS

PREVIOUS PAGE
Ranger Lisa Marks stands guard on paintings in Kakadu National Park. As a condition of lease for the park, the traditional owners require a ranger to be present during visiting hours to protect the rock paintings, which are thousands of years old. KAKADU NT

Adam Pepper, Kim Sheebob and Jarrad Burdett ride home past Uluru
after a swim at the new Residents' Pool at Ayers Rock Resort. ULURU, NT

Houseboats in Mountain Bay for the Earthcore Festival. LAKE EILDON, VIC

Mark Williams and 'Spinny'.
MOUNT PARRY, NSW

**Serious business – hunters
Rob, Shane, Scott and Peter.**
MOUNT PARRY, NSW

JOANNE FELK

■ Ready for the shearing shed? HEATHCOTE, VIC

■ At 'Redcliffe', a superfine wool property owned by husband and wife Miles Cockington and Allyson Parsons, two–year–old Henry approaches a very suspicious ewe with some lupins. 'Redcliffe' is in very severe drought – the staple diet of the sheep is the bluebush seen in the background. NEAR BURRA, SA

MICHAEL COYNE

ROBERT MCFARLANE

Tea time for Jack Otway. Prospector and miner, Jack has been working his lease for years. He re—dug the 20m shaft and put in a 13m crosscut with a pick and shovel, working by the light of a single candle. Jack reckons at 85 he's better off doing this than sitting at home doing nothing! KALGOORLIE, WA

A dairy farmer at Meeniyan, Keith Jeffrey feeds his cows once a day with hay containing clover and fog grass. He worries about genetically modified engineering as he believes nature can always adapt itself to compensate for any changes. He chooses not to artificially inseminate his herd and on 140 acres he runs 110 Jersey milking cows who produce top quality milk. SOUTH GIPPSLAND, VIC

■ Time out for farmer Tom Dowd. MOUNT CAMEL, VIC

MICHAEL COYNE

■ Organic dairy farmers Scott and Suzanne
Whiteman do not use any chemicals on their dairy
farm at Mardan. Any animal health problems are dealt
with by using vitamin and mineral supplements – they
occasionally need to use penicillin and work with a
homeopathic vet. Scott is getting better production per
cow, outproducing other farms with similar acreage,
and there is no degrading of the animal or the soil.
SOUTH GIPPSLAND, VIC

■ With no international cricket on New Year's Day, campers head for the beach for their own game. ROSEBUD, VIC

GARY LEWIS

■ VB seems to be the choice at Mt Erskine River camping grounds and caravan park. LORNE, VIC

RENNIE ELLIS

DAVID SIMMONDS

DAVID SIMMONDS

■ Ditchley Park, home of Otway Cricket Club.

Left, local umpire Robert 'Monty' Montgomery.
BEECH FOREST, VIC

131

■ Cable Beach.
BROOME, WA

PETER HASSON

■ Stuart Oastler fishes
and Lynn Smith provides
the paddle power.
KAKADU NATIONAL PARK, NT

JEAN-PAUL FERRERO

132

To bring a smile to the face of all who enjoy a succulent cray!
KATHERINE BAY, ROTTNEST ISLAND, WA

TRISH AINSLIE

■ Golfers share the course with kangaroos at Anglesea Golf Club.
ANGLESEA, VIC

RENNIE ELLIS

■ Charlie the buffalo, of 'Crocodile Dundee' fame,
with 'Blue' Robins, at the Adelaide River Pub.
Weighing in at one tonne, Charlie is 26 years old and
has his original horns with a total span of 2.25 metres.
STUART HIGHWAY, NT

DANIEL LINET

■ Pro Hart fires up the paint cannon and slingshot for the finishing touches to his first painting of the new millennium.
BROKEN HILL, NSW

■ The famous Palace Hotel where 'Priscilla Queen of the Desert' was filmed – owner Mario with the hand–painted murals that cover all the hotel walls. BROKEN HILL, NSW

■ Born 1899, Ernst Charles Peddell, a veteran of both World Wars, has lived in three centuries. Ernie enlisted in the 1st AIF in 1917 at the age of 17 and served in France and Belgium. In WWII, he was one of the Rats of Tobruk and also served in New Guinea. His room at the RSL Retirement Hostel is decorated with a letter from the Prime Minister, his Medal of Honor citation from the French Government and his Masonic Lodge long service award. Recently, Ernie received a notice from the Sheriff's Office to say he may be called for jury duty. "I don't mind, but I'm a little hard of hearing, so they will have to speak up a bit," he says with a smile. YASS, NSW

GRAHAM GITTINS

MONICA NAPPER

■ Light Horse Veteran of World War I, Thomas Robinson (right), and Malcolm Carter, World War II veteran. Thomas Robinson was born in 1897 at Victor Harbor. Posted to the First Light Horse in 1916 he served in Cyclist Battalions and was awarded a number of medals. He later held every South Australian cycling record from half–mile to 100 miles.

Note: As at 1.1.2000 there were four known Australian WW1 veterans living in S.A. and 34 WW1 veterans in Australia.

Malcolm Carter spent his 21st birthday in Tobruk under siege. After being relieved by the Polish Army, his battalion returned to Egypt and was sent to Syria to prepare for El Alamein. During the 'big push' Mr Carter was wounded and had his leg amputated in hospital in Alexandria. He is President of the Limbless Soldiers of S.A. WEST BEACH, SA

The music programme for the day – Glenlyon Sports Day. GLENLYON, VIC

Preferred mode of transport on Rottnest Island. WA

JOANNE FELK

■ Ken Arundell prepares a day's
feed for his pigs at 'Mount One Tree'.
Right, Ken and wife Helen with Buddy
on their verandah. MOUNT PARRY, NSW

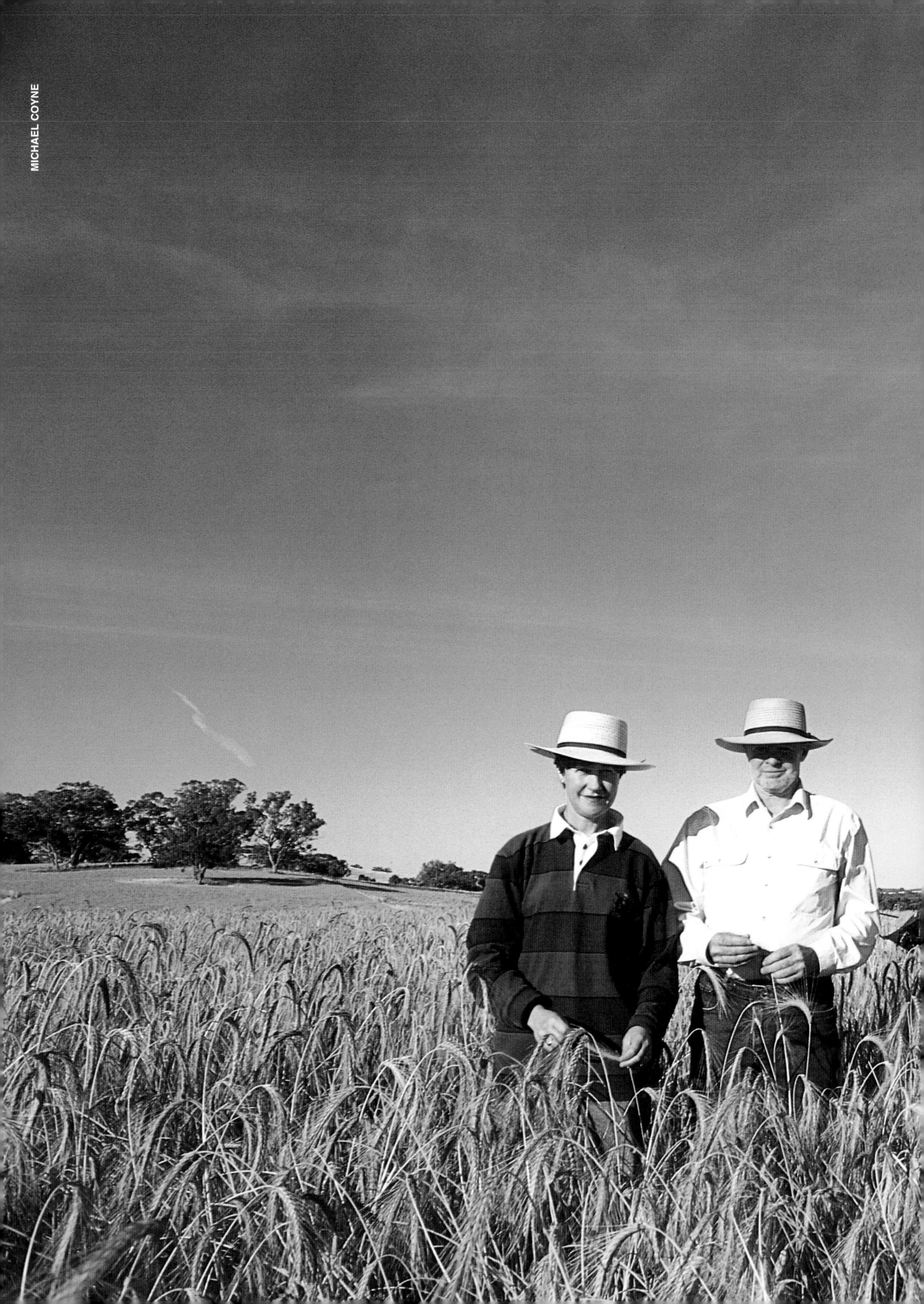

MICHAEL COYNE

Farmers Tom and Juliet Dowd in grainfield. MOUNT CAMEL, VIC

■ What lies ahead?
Circular Quay.
SYDNEY, NSW

■ Checking e–mail from
home at 'Global Gossip'
internet café. Chris and
Jeremy from Ohio, (with
US forces based in
Belgium), and Sarah,
Katherine and Luke
(foreground) from Cairns.
CAIRNS, QLD

There'll always be an England! SYDNEY, NSW

DAVID DARE PARKER

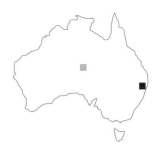

TIM GEORGESON

■ Koori kids . NIMBIN, NSW

■ Modern oasis? AYERS ROCK RESORT, NT

■ They're racing!
Wallabadah Picnic Races.
WALLABADAH, NSW

TONY BEE

■ Checking the odds at
Hanging Rock Races.
HANGING ROCK, VIC

MICHAEL COYNE

Celebrating her
selection for the
marching band at
the Sydney Olympic
Games, Ebony
Collins on Quincy.
LEONGATHA, VIC

Recent immigrants to Australia, Americans Kamala and Neil Amberose, with Jonah
(6) and Malaka (8) on their organic chicken and egg farm in Wilsons Creek. When
they bought the 70 acres it came with 800 chooks, two cats and a dog: "A complete
change of lifestyle from Northern California," says Kamala. MULLUMBIMBY, NSW

Jessica Jacobson (11)

Yoshi Cameron-Bradley (11)

We supplied a number of children
with Fujicolor QuickSnap Super 800
single-use cameras on the day.
These are some of the results.

Jasper Parker Trenfield (12)

Leah Billing (11)

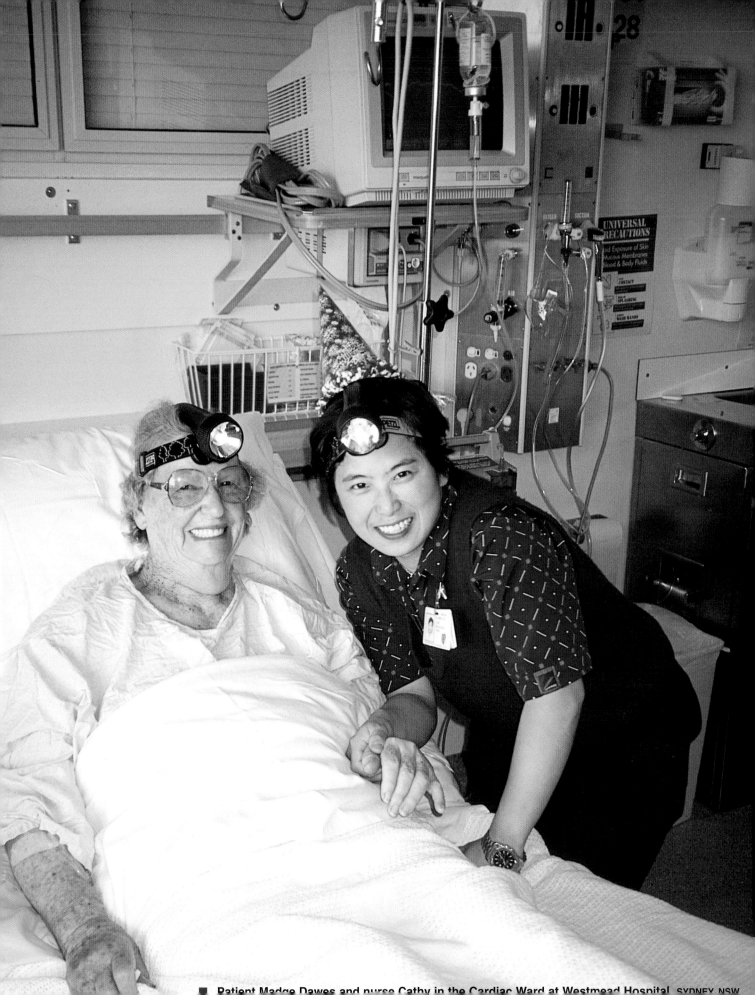

Patient Madge Dawes and nurse Cathy in the Cardiac Ward at Westmead Hospital, SYDNEY, NSW

BRIAN CASSEY

▪ Trouble times seven! The first day of the new century saw Leisha Kennedy trying to occupy her extraordinary family of a set of triplets, a set of twins and two older boys. CAIRNS, QLD

■ "Can we help you?" Betty Chapman (left) and Barbara Smart at Tamworth Information Centre. Representing the country music capital of Australia, the Centre is shaped like a guitar!
TAMWORTH, NSW

■ Lions Club members watch as a time capsule buried in 1973 is raised from the ground.
BROKEN HILL, NSW

JOANNE FELK

DANIEL LINET

JAKE JACOBSON

■ Matthew Stephenson wins the 2000 Burnie Gift at the New Year's Day Carnival. BURNIE, TAS

■ English–born Heather and Stephen Pyatt now live on the Gold Coast but continue some quaint English seaside traditions. NORTHCLIFFE BEACH, QLD

RICHARD CAMPION

■ Marriage celebration on the first day of a new millennium – Stephanie Choo and Victor Dio at St Patricks Cathedral, photographer from Fidelity Studios.
MELBOURNE, VIC

KIM TONELLI

■ Khaled and
Mamdouha Dannan
at home celebrating
Ramadan, the ninth
month of the Muslim
lunar calendar. Their
family all came
together to break
their fast at 8:10pm

JOANNE SAAD

Ramadan: prayer time in
Muslim Mosque, men's
and women's sections.

JOANNE SAAD

The Cromack family at sunset on 1.1.2000
after enjoying fish and chips on the beach.
ST. KILDA BEACH, VIC

■ Solving the problem of who's going to ride – l to r: Andrea Broadbent with daughters Anna (1), Lauren (5) and Megan (3). GLENELG, SA

TONY LEWIS

■ Mudbath! BAFFLE CREEK, QLD

■ Plum picking at an ashram – this Satyananda Yoga based retreat runs a bush regeneration programme in an effort to eliminate introduced species.
MANGROVE MOUNTAIN, NSW

BRUCE HART

■ Miles Cockington and wife Allyson with Allyson's parents, Marie and Wolford Parsons.
PT VINCENT, SA

ROBERT MCFARLANE

■ A man's best friend. Len Baeur on his farm. WINFIELD, QLD

■ Cottesloe Beach. PERTH, WA

ROEL LOOPERS

■ Outside Maid
Marion's General Store
on the Great Ocean
Road: Ryan Evans,
Marvin de la Cruz, Chris
Bott, Clinton Evans and
Francois Sappleton.
ANGLESEA, VIC

■ Sergeant Peter
Flanders and Senior
Constable Jim Murphy
seem more interested in
inspecting this
preproduction Ultima
sports car than booking
the driver. BRISBANE, QLD

5:35pm. The entire population of Kookynie turns out for a portrait. In the bush north of Kalgoorlie, it is one of the most isolated settlements in the country, its residents living in a ghost town. At the turn of the last century, it had a population of 20,000, several hotels, breweries, a hospital, several brass bands and many hopeful prospectors and mine workers. All that remains is a small row of shops, the Grand Hotel and a couple of old homes which used to be miners' shacks.
KOOKYNIE, WA

■ It's been a long night and a hard day and beds are hard to come by.
WALLABADAH, NSW

TONY BEE

■ Marisa Ferraz is truly one of Broome's entrepreneurs. She came to the area at the age of 17 and worked in a café which she subsequently purchased. A few years later, she also purchased Sun Pictures, 'the oldest operating picture gardens in the world'. She would collect the door takings for the theatre then run across the street to cook in her café. When asked to comment on Broome and her life: "There's nothing you can say… it is just magic!" BROOME, WA

■ The Grand Hotel is Kookynie's social centre. The bar attracts prospectors tired of the heat and flies. Bob Harry (in hat) has just arrived after driving the 1200km virtually non–stop from Alice Springs along the Gunbarrel Highway. Bob comes to Kookynie during the wet season, finding it a better spot at this time of year than his Queensland home town of Cooktown. He is showing his collection of gold nuggets to Simon Thornton (extreme left), young prospector Luke Duncan, Stacey Thornton (leaning on left of counter) and Lyn Duncan (right). KOOKYNIE, WA

■ Below, high tea at the Windsor Hotel. Maitre d', Zoran Angelovski, chats with guests. Left, John Ridge, hotel doorman.
MELBOURNE, VIC

Father and son watch the sun set on the first day of the century. DOVER HEIGHTS, NSW

■ Unusually inclement weather produces an almost deserted Bondi Beach. SYDNEY, NSW

MICHAEL AMENDOLIA

■ Three generations of the Kelly family celebrate the new year with a barbecue at the Toowoomba Waterbird Habitat Park. TOOWOOMBA, QLD

■ Sunset on 1.1.2000: Ben and Amanda Treloar
and two–year–old George make up the total
population of Thistle Island, where they farm sheep
and caretake the island. Nearest town: Port Lincoln.
SPENCER GULF, OFF THE COAST OF EYRE PENINSULA, SA

MATT TURNER

■ E.J. Leonard at 'Amarna'.
MOUNT PARRY, NSW

■ Women gather on the beach with hundreds of flowers which they are offering to the sea in a rather mysterious ceremony of their own making. BYRON BAY, NSW

■ Rex Hunt eat your heart out!
Trout fishing at Launceston Lakes.
LAUNCESTON TAS

■ In spite of cloud cover, which means no red rock at sunset, everyone still enjoys the experience. ULURU, NT

BILL BACHMAN

■ Mansfield Millennium Balloon Festival, features the 'Nightglow Twelve' which includes special–shaped balloons using their gas burners individually to illuminate the colourful balloons from the inside. MANSFIELD, VIC

■ Dusk at the 12 Apostles, Port Campbell National Park.
GREAT OCEAN ROAD, VIC

Lantern procession at Woodford Folk Festival on the first night of the new year. The Woodford Festival is a huge, multi-cultural event lasting more than a week with an attendance of around 84,000. Over 1500 people worked on making the lanterns carried in the Fire Festival lantern procession. MALENY, QLD

TRISH AINSLEY

ROBYN BINGHAM

MICHAEL COYNE

MICHAEL AMENDOLIA

MERVYN BISHOP

GRAHAM BURSTOW

JEAN-PAUL FERRERO

GARY BLINCO

RICHARD CAMPION

TREVERN DAWES

BILL BACHMAN

BRIAN CASSEY

NEALE DUCKWORTH

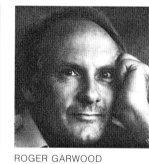

ROGER GARWOOD

TONY BEE

ANDREW CHAPMAN

TIM GEORGESON

JAMES BRAUND

RENNIE ELLIS

TRISH AINSLEY

A recent joint winner of the Gold Corporation prize for the best image depicting the gold mining industry. Trish works as a freelance photo-journalist and has teamed up with Roger Garwood on several book projects, including *Land's Edge* (with Tim Winton), and *Fremantle – Life in the Port City.*

MICHAEL AMENDOLIA

Worked as a staff photographer for News Ltd for 15 years covering sports, news, politics and features, his assignments including many famous personages. Between 1992 and 1994 Michael photographed for the Fred Hollows book *Seeing is Believing* in Viet Nam, Nepal, Eritrea and Torres Strait Islands. He was awarded a first prize at World Press Photo Awards in Amsterdam in 1999 for his story on cataract blindness. As a freelance he has photographed for almost all major Australian magazines as well as for German and English newspapers.

BILL BACHMAN

Born in the United States, Bill has lived in Australia since 1973. An award winning freelance photojournalist, he has contributed articles and photographs to a wide variety of books and magazines around the world. He has held a number of solo exhibitions and is the author of several successful books.

TONY BEE

Acclaimed award-winning photographer, with numerous exhibitions to his credit, photography has always been his passion. He has a broad spectrum of national and international clientele. Operating from Brisbane, Tony says he always seeks *"clarity, depth and mood."*

ROBYN BINGHAM

One of a new generation in the contemporary field, Robyn specialises as a people photographer, with award winning portraits to her credit. Currently experimenting in the digital field, she also lectures and judges both locally and interstate.

MERVYN BISHOP

Commenced as a cadet at *The Sydney Morning Herald* becoming Australia's first Aboriginal press photographer. Later he moved to the Department of Aboriginal Affairs as photographer, before moving back to the *Herald* until 1986. He completed his Associate Diploma of Adult Education in 1989, after which he taught photography at both Tranby College and the Eora Centre. Mervyn held his first solo exhibition in 1991 and his work is now widely exhibited, documenting both indigenous and dominant cultures.

GARY BLINCO

Was motivated by the beauty of New Zealand scenery to undertake a diploma in photography. Having worked in the mining industry, it was a natural for him to pursue this field as a source of images. With his photographer wife, he operates a commercial studio in Kalgoorlie.

JAMES BRAUND

Is an editorial photographer specialising in portraits and features. After working for many years in London for the Brtish Film Institute, he relocated to Melbourne, where he freelances for the Fairfax Group. His images appear in several magazines including *Good Weekend, Inside Sport, Australian Way* and *The Financial Review Magazine.*

GRAHAM BURSTOW

Past President of the Australian Photographic Society and author of *Touch Me,* a book of photographic images, an active exhibitor, judge and lecturer, he has prints in many collections and has held numerous one-man and joint exhibitions in Australia and overseas.

RICHARD CAMPION

Known to his confreres as Tommy, he began his career with the *Northern Star* in Lismore then moved on to newspapers such as *The Townsville Star* and *The Courier Mail.* He worked for over 20 years for News Ltd until the closure of *The Sunday Sun* and *Daily Sun,* when he relocated to the Gold Coast. He now freelances for national and overseas publications.

BRIAN CASSEY

Writes: "First camera cost me two and sixpence in Woolworths and a twist of a coin in a slot was needed to open it. I was 11 at the time. First professional subjects were at Charlton Athletic Football Club in London. Left the UK for Australia in 1973, ended up in tropical Cairns where I expanded my sports photography base to include news and features. Won the inaugural Adidas/Kodak Sports Photo of the Year in 1985 and have managed to snaffle a fair sprinkling of awards since for both news and sports photographs."

ANDREW CHAPMAN

Emerged from Prahran CAE with honours and the Agfa Award for Printing Excellence. He worked as a newspaper photographer for a number of years before setting up on his own, where he caters for corporate clients and major magazines. He documents lifestyles and is currently working on political images and portraits of individuals.

MICHAEL COYNE

Has worked for 25 years as a photojournalist, covering wars, revolutions and international events all over the world. His work has appeared in almost all major newspapers and journals and been recognised by numerous national and international awards. He is contracted to the prestigious Black Star agency, has worked on a number of *Day in the Life...* projects and was both a photographer and director of photography on *Planet Vegas,* the award winning book.

TREVERN DAWES

Has five photo/travel books published in Australia and New Zealand, numerous articles for major travel magazines, held several one-man exhibitions and also found time to teach photography. He is well represented at photo agencies and specialises in landscape photography, valuing the tranquillity of the outback.

NEALE DUCKWORTH

A staff photographer at *The Melbourne Age,* he resigned in 1987 to work freelance in New York, returning to Melbourne in 1990. His documentary *Connies,* depicting the last of Melbourne's tram conductors, was shown during 1999 at the State Library of Victoria. His work appears in collections such as the Australian Portrait Gallery and the Fuji/ACMP collection.

RENNIE ELLIS

Is an image junky and compulsive photographer who delights in chronicling popular culture and is intrigued by the quirkiness of human behaviour, especially when it ventures into the realms of the erotic, exotic and esoteric. He has 17 books to his credit, *Life's Still a Beach* being the most recent. His photographs have been exhibited around the world and included in important collections, including those of the National Gallery of Australia and France's Bibliotheque Nationale.

JOANNE FELK

Is a Newcastle based photographer with over 15 years' experience in the photographic industry, with major clients in commercial, industrial and portraiture. She has received many awards, including AIPP NSW Professional Photographer of the Year for 1998 and 1999.

JEAN-PAUL FERRERO

Born in France, Jean-Paul showed an early interest in nature and since 1972 has spent his life photographing it. He moved to Australia in 1982. His pictures have been published by most major magazines in the world and he is the founder of Auscape International, a photo library based in Sydney

ROGER GARWOOD

Was formerly staff photographer with *Paris Match* and now freelances for various magazines. He works with Trish Ainslee, specialising in changing lifestyles and has published nine books with her, including *Off Like Flies,* the definitive book about the last of Australia's traditional gold prospectors, and *'til She Dropped Her Strides* which illustrates the lifestyle of the Kimberley.

TIM GEORGESON

Was born in Singapore and now lives in Sydney. Tim specialises in environmental portraiture and social documentary photography. His recent assignments include post-tsunami reportage in Papua New Guinea, pre-war coverage in Kosovo, documentation of Azeri refugees in Azerbaijan and a personal project with his journalist wife, Caia, documenting aspects of religious life as well as Tibetan refugees in India. He had his first solo exhibition in March 1999 at Sydney's Art House Gallery.

GRAHAM GITTINS

TERRY KNIGHT

TONY LEWIS

ANDREW MATHIESON

RACHEL HARRIS

PHILIP KURUVITA

LEON MEAD

PHILIP GOSTELOW

PETER HASSON

DANIEL LINET

ROBERT GRAY

MICHAEL LANGFORD

ROEL LOOPERS

GRAHAM MONRO

PATRICK HAMILTON

ROBERT MCFARLANE

CAROLYN JOHNS

GARY LEWIS

JEFF MOORFOOT

GRAHAM GITTINS

Photographing and writing about politicians, historic vehicles and Australian heritage, history and lifestyle, has kept this Canberra based photojournalist busy for the past 30 years. He was the inaugural winner of the Kodak/National Trust of Australia (ACT) Heritage photographic competition, and he also photographed, very successfully, for *Christmas in Australia.*

PHILIP GOSTELOW

Was born in Perth where he took a degree in architecture. He lived in North America developing an interest in photography which continued with his five years in Tokyo. He now lives in the Blue Mountains with his work appearing regularly in major Australian publications. His portrait and documentary work have been featured by international news magazines in the UK and Japan, where he has held a number of exhibitions.

ROBERT GRAY

Is one of Australia's most experienced photographers, dividing his time between Cairns and Brisbane. He undertakes work for corporate, tourism and editorial clients in areas as diverse as Papua New Guinea and Melbourne. He began his career in newspapers, has lived and worked in Hong Kong and has won awards for sports photography. He is a past national president of the AIPP.

PATRICK HAMILTON

A staff photographer with *The Australian* newspaper for the past 10 years, covering events as diverse as royal tours, to HIV in PNG. His work appears in other publications including *Time, Bulletin, Inside Sport, Reuters.* Patrick is currently completing a black and white retro exhibition due late 2000. He was winner of the 1998 Walkley Award for coverage of the tidal wave which struck Northern PNG last year, and its aftermath.

DAVID HANCOCK

Has worked in the top end as a freelance writer and photographer since 1987 and operates Sky Scans Photo Library with his spouse. He enjoys the freedom and space of the region and being able to work every day of the year that he wants to.

RACHEL HARRIS

Is one of Adelaide's more sought after photographers, especially well known in the music scene with award winning CD covers. Her work encompasses the whole gamut from commercial to arts to photo-journalism.

PETER HASSON

Has worked as a professional photographer for the past 10 years, being extensively published throughout Australia and overseas.
He has received several awards and is now state president for Western Australia of the AIPP.

JAKE JACOBSON

Photographing for the past 10 years, Jake has collected several gold awards. He runs a photographic studio in Ulverstone, Tasmania.

CAROLYN JOHNS

Has been a professional photographer for 22 years, working in the areas of corporate, reportage, advertising, tourism, portraiture, documentary, animals and landscape. Caroline has worked for an impressive list of major overseas publications. Film stills and specials include *Mad Max II, Babe* and *Babe – Pig in the City.* She has co-directed and co-produced a video in partnership with the Australian Youth Parliament for the Environment, as well as organising national media for their conference in Canberra and ongoing projects.

TERRY KNIGHT

Combines photography, pharmaceutical science, journalism and teaching photo design. Best known for his wilderness and outback landscape work, he has held solo exhibitions in the UK and Australia and has been published in numerous national magazines and books. Corporate, construction and landscape assignments take Terry throughout S.E. Asia, Europe and Australia. He also lectures and is a long time supporter of the arts.

PHILIP KURUVITA

Says: "*A Day in the Life of Australia* was the first photographic book I owned. Inscribed by my father it simply read *To our photo catcher, love Mum and Dad 24/12/81.*" Eighteen years on, with his own photographic studio in Tasmania, Philip has received several major awards. "The wheel has come full circle. The letter confirming my involvement in this project arrived on the second anniversary of Dad's death – I know he would be pleased."

MICHAEL LANGFORD

Has a huge list of awards and accomplishments in the industry in both Australia and New Zealand. He was one of the participants in the original *A Day in the Life of New Zealand* in 1983 and then progressed to titles like *Han Suyin's China, Korea – Land of the Morning Calm* and *The Mount Cook Book.* He is much in demand as a lecturer and photographic judge.

GARY LEWIS

His career as a photographer began when he won four sections in a world-wide Pentax competition. He has operated his own travel photography business for over 20 years with his work appearing in brochures, calendars, books, magazines and airline publicity. He is also particularly noted for his sports and nature photography.

TONY LEWIS

Began his career as a photographer in 1978 as a cadet on *The News* in Adelaide. He moved to *The Advertiser* and then to London to work on Fleet Street. On his return to Australia, Tony joined *The Sydney Morning Herald* before returning to Adelaide where he has been *The Australian's* bureau photographer since 1988.

DANIEL LINET

Since his arrival in Australia from his native Ukraine, Daniel has always, in one way or another, been involved in the arts. From his inner-Sydney studio, he concentrates on fashion and commercial assignments. Reportage/photojournalism has always been a passion, which has led to extensive travels locally and abroad. He has documented life from local Sydney streets to the red light districts of Bombay.

ROEL LOOPERS

Was born in Holland and worked in Germany for many years, his work appearing in dailies, magazines and major agencies. He migrated to Australia and as a freelance has photographed for architects, designers, mining and industrial companies, government departments and advertising agencies. His work is exhibited extensively in Australia and Europe and is held in corporate and private collections.

ROBERT McFARLANE

Has freelanced as a photo-journalist in Australia for three decades, except for 1970-73 when he photographed for *The Daily Telegraph, The Sunday Times* and *Nova* magazine in London. He has maintained a consistent passion for documenting performance in film and theatre and describes himself as a 'compulsive diarist'. He writes regularly on photography and other subjects.

ANDREW MATHIESON

A photography enthusiast for most of his formative years, Andrew went on to gain professional qualifications. A move back to Katherine to establish his business coincided with the unprecedented Australia Day 1998 floods. After clearing up, he has proceeded undeterred and considers participation in this project one of the most satisfying in which to be involved.

LEON MEAD

Grew up in Goolwa on the Murray. Initially held a cadetship at *Victor Harbour Times* finishing at *The Adelaide News.* Four years at *The Stock Journal* saw Leon get back to his roots with country S.A. people. He is currently a senior photographer and pictorial editor with *The Advertiser* in Adelaide.

MARCO MONA

Born in Italy, Marco first approached photographic studies as a fun way of relieving the tedium of an interpreting and translating degree. He now runs his own Perth studio and divides his time between commercial and advertising photography and art-directing for film and television.

GRAHAM MONRO

Is a highly regarded people and locations photographer based in Sydney. Extensively awarded both nationally and internationally, his work is regularly featured in the elite Fuji ASMP collections. He is heavily involved in negotiation and licensing workshops and assistance to photography students, putting something back into the industry.

JEFF MOORFOOT

A Geelong native, Jeff was a late starter in photography but has succeeded in a hurry. He shoots mainly in the commercial/advertising field and also lectures part time. He has held several exhibitions and says he is yet to decide what he wants to be when he grows up.

FIONA MORRIS

ROGER SCOTT

PETER SOLNESS

DAVID DARE PARKER

RUSSELL SHAKESPEARE

PENNY TWEEDIE

MONICA NAPPER

DOUG SPOWART

BRAD RIMMER

DAVID SIMMONDS

ROB WALLS

PETER O'HALLORAN

JOANNE SAAD

KIM TONELLI

SORREL WILBY

STUART OWEN-FOX

BARRY SKIPSEY

MATT TURNER

FIONA MORRIS

Received a scholarship in 1995 to study at the International Centre for Photography in New York. Predominantly a documentary photographer, Fiona's work has been exhibited both locally and internationally. She has been working on a freelance basis for the last two years and currently is working at the Australian Centre for Photography in Sydney.

BILL MOSELEY

Was photographer to the Australian Opera and the Australian Ballet in the '70s. He has participated in group shows as the Opera House, Nelson Street Gallery and the TAP Gallery. He has received a number of awards and held a residency at the Bemis Contemporary Art Center in Omaha, Nebraska. His work is held in collections in Sydney, Berlin and Omahu.

MONICA NAPPER

Developed her hobby into a career, with her work appearing in numerous overseas magazines, newspapers and books before settling in Adelaide. She works for both the mainstream press and commercial clients.

PETER O'HALLORAN

Has recorded the community around him for over 30 years. A former Press Photographer of the Year, Peter displays a sensitive eye and has specialised in photographing people, whether it be in the corporate world or for newspapers.

STUART OWEN-FOX

Covered Byron Bay for *A Day in the Life of Australia* in 1981. His pictures have appeared in more than 200 books, hundreds of magazines and posters, and on postage stamps. He has been a professional photographer for 40 years.

DAVID DARE PARKER

Australian based photo-journalist, David has photographed for many national and international publications and worked on photo essays throughout Asia, Middle East and Europe. A Walkley Award winner, his work is represented by l'Agence Vu in Paris and Wildlight Photo Agency in Sydney. His total list of awards is much too extensive to mention as are the publications that have carried his work. His credits with the performing arts reflect his artistic sensitivity.

BRAD RIMMER

Is a Perth based freelance photographer, born in the wheat-belt town of Wyalkatchem. Apart from his commercial work, Brad uses photography as his artistic medium, recent projects including pin hole photos of Romania and documenting China with a plastic toy camera.

JOANNE SAAD

Studied at the College of Fine Art, University of NSW. To date she has produced three major bodies of work, exhibited nationally and internationally with her work purchased by galleries and museums. She has worked in North Africa, Middle East and Europe and currently freelances in Sydney.

PETER SANDERSON

Born in Weiz, Austria, Peter immigrated to Australia with his parents in 1956. His father gave him his first camera at the age of 11 and his passion for photography began. For many years Peter's professional background was Applied Science and photography his main hobby. When he moved to the Gold Coast in 1989, he took up professional photography and he now enjoys shooting what most other photographers try to avoid, weddings, animals and children.

ROGER SCOTT

Has been described as "the Cartier-Bresson of Australia" with his innate ability to capture the right moment, his work exhibiting a singular humour, irony and sensitivity. A Visual Arts Board grant took him to the US, since when he has held a number of one-man exhibitions.

RUSSELL SHAKESPEARE

His work appears every week in *The Australian Magazine*, having worked previously for the *Australian*. A first class photo-journalist of the new breed, in 1994 he was awarded the Nikon News Photographer of the Year and in 1995 won a Walkley Award for News Photography.

DAVID SIMMONDS

Born in Zimbabwe, David's family migrated to Australia in 1964. His passion for photography took him firstly to Adelaide and then to Melbourne. He has over 20 years experience in the industry and his work is widely published. He is the 1999 Victorian Commercial and Industrial Photographer of the Year and in that year was runner up in the same category for the whole of Australia.

BARRY SKIPSEY

Love of the outback and his participation in its lifestyle through various occupations, caused him to settle in Alice Springs and concentrate on photography. Barry is in great demand from overseas publications as well as Australian government departments, weeklies, dailies and tour operators. His empathy with Aboriginal culture and his readiness to camp out in the scrub gives his work great reality. He is also a most accomplished guitarist, singer-songwriter, perhaps best known for his *"You'll never never know if you never never go."*

PETER SOLNESS

Has over 20 years' experience in editorial and corporate photography. He has worked for most major Australian newspapers and magazines as well as US, European and Asian publications. Peter has been principal photographer on eight books and participated in many group projects and exhibitions.

DOUG SPOWART

From modest beginnings in the late 60's with involvement in camera clubs, Doug has gone on to receive acclaim and awards. With his mother, Ruby, he operated the Art Imagery Gallery from 1980 to 1995. He is currently employed by the South Queensland Institute of Tafe and has lectured at tertiary level on photography since 1997. Five times the recipient of the AIPP Queensland Professional Photographer of the Year award, he has been a staunch supporter of the industry at all levels.

KIM TONELLI

After graduating in 1989, Kim went overseas and worked in over 30 cities. She photographed in the highly competitive British music and entertainment field, mostly on editorial and record sleeves with such as the Rolling Stones and Oasis. She is now based in Melbourne.

MATT TURNER

Is an Adelaide based freelance photographer, having worked from 1986 at The News until its closure in 1992. He has since specialised in magazine and press work, his pictures appearing regularly in *The Australian*. Matt also specialises in sports photography.

PENNY TWEEDIE

A freelance photo-journalist, Penny has worked on assignments in 69 countries for almost all major world magazines and non-government organisations such as Save the Children and Oxfam, covering everything from wars, famines, events, people in every predicament to celebrities, company reports and education. She worked on *A Day in the Life of Australia* and also ... *USA*. She has been a major contributor to numerous books and is known in Australia for her two books on the Australian Aborigines, most recently *Spirit of Arnhem Land*.

ROB WALLS

From his base on the lower slopes of Mt Wellington in Hobart, Rob specialises in editorial, corporate and illustrative photography. His experience covers the gamut from childbirth to war. When not working on assignment for mainland and international publications, he teaches photojournalism to students around the world through the Australian College of Journalism.

SORREL WILBY

A 17,000km bike ride across Asia, a 3000km solo trek across Tibet, the world's first complete traverse of the Himalayas, ascents of all the highest peaks on the African continent and numerous journeys throughout Australia have inspired Sorrel's writing and photography for nearly 20 years. Her work has appeared in close to 100 magazines and newspapers around the world. She has had seven books published, the most recent being *Images from the Wild Side*, a lavish collection of photographs from her many explorations. Sorrel is currently working as a reporter for Chanel 9's travel programme *Getaway*.

Also
BRUCE HART
GRANT KEIGHLEY
MATT NETTHEIM
LYN WHITFIELD-KING

Notes from Malcolm McGregor

SOME MELBOURNE
PARTICIPANTS

This book has been twelve months in the planning. Travelling the country viewing portfolios, explaining the concept, discussing likely subjects and arranging permissions can be a long drawn out, and at times frustrating task. But without exception we met with nothing but courtesy and enthusiasm. The photographic industry contains some wonderful characters. So great was the response that we were inundated with offers from prospective participants and it proved an embarrassment to have to turn talented people away.

We determined that, unlike similar one-day projects, we would engage only Australian photographers, producing shots of Australians for Australia - all local people covering the country from Hobart to Darwin, from Cairns to Broome, from Adelaide to Alice. Of course, like all projects of this magnitude, the unexpected always occurs. People dropped in and out, Timor occurred, millennial tasks overseas called, Kosovo and Grozny beckoned, and always somebody with excellent credentials stepped in.

A SYDNEY BRIEFING

On the day, the weather was unkind in many regions - sunrises at Mt Wellington and Cape Byron were scarcely visible. Nevertheless, readers will be able to judge for themselves how well 65 talented photographers overcame the day's problems.

From about 25,000 shots, we have chosen 200 to represent for history the state of our nation when we stepped over the threshold into the 21st century. Let history be our judge.

Our hope is that this visual record will illustrate the diversity of our nation amongst its celebrations, and that there is room for all points of view, nationalities, customs and lifestyles in a vibrant democracy.

For my part, I thank all the photographers for their enthusiasm and hard work, some of them going without sleep for 36 hours; Mark and Irene Garner for their unfailing understanding, tremendous skill and for their hospitality; Juliet Rogers, Hazel Flynn and the staff of Random House for making our job so much easier; Joe Kosac, Virginia and Craig McGregor, Robin and Neil Batchelor, Pam Kent, and the hundreds of Australians like Shane and Sue O'Sullivan at 'Killara Park' who so willingly assisted our photographers.

200